Fire Up Your Life Now!

Dianne —
All the best to our
favorite accountant!
Warmest —
Barbara + Allan

Fire Up Your Life Now!

25
Secrets
for Creating
the Life You Really Want

Allan and Barbara Kenyon

iUniverse, Inc.
New York Bloomington Shanghai

Fire Up Your Life Now!
25 Secrets for Creating the Life You Really Want

iUniverse books may be ordered through booksellers or by contacting:

iUniverse
1663 Liberty Drive
Bloomington, IN 47403
www.iuniverse.com
1-800-Authors (1-800-288-4677)

Because of the dynamic nature of the Internet, any Web addresses or links contained in this book may have changed since publication and may no longer be valid.

The views expressed in this work are solely those of the author and do not necessarily reflect the views of the publisher, and the publisher hereby disclaims any responsibility for them.

ISBN: 978-0-595-43514-2 (pbk)
ISBN: 978-0-595-87840-6 (ebk)

Printed in the United States of America

To three
of the most fired up people we know,
our happy, motivated, enthusiastic children:
Todd Kenyon, Jordan Kenyon, Meredith Kenyon

To Dad/Grandpa
Hy Kaplan.
You live each day with optimism and humor,
and inspire us to do the same.

Contents

Introduction

Welcome and thank you for choosing *Fire Up Your Life Now!* As you read through the pages, you will discover secrets that can change your life. Why do we call these ideas secrets when nearly everything you want to know is available in a library or on the Internet? The answer is simple: So many people are not living a fired up, fulfilled life, and these secrets appear to be unused.

Having coached several thousand people, we have learned, with certainty, that people are capable, competent, and filled with unlimited potential. You have within you everything you will ever need to become whatever you choose. In this book, you will read stories about our clients and how they made improvements to their lives. We have changed their names, and we have been granted permission to use their confidential stories.

The secrets in this book are not a quick fix approach. This is not a drive-in window where you say, "I'll take the Self-Confidence Special and Super-Size it." Although, when you begin to change your thinking and your actions, you will be amazed at the speed of your progress. You will begin to see what is possible for you.

The only qualification you need to start this journey is to show up. There is nothing to pack. No supplies are needed. Just bring yourself and your unlimited potential. You are not too old. You are not too young. You are just right.

We will ask you questions to help you become clear as to what you really, really want. You will be asked to think about what is blocking you from living your dream life now. At the end of each secret you will find a simple exercise that will help you put the secret into action to eliminate those blocks.

There is no wrong way to experience this book. Please do not be overwhelmed by the number of secrets. They stand alone so you can open the book to any secret and receive a powerful benefit. Take your time with each secret. When a secret stirs you and speaks to you, dive into it and make it yours. Allow the benefits to surface within you.

One of our favorite authors and coaches, Mike Dooley, says, "*The number one reason most people don't start what they want to start is because they think their simple, little efforts won't even dent the mountain they wish to move. But little do they know that's exactly how the mountain was formed.*"

Our goal is to help you jar yourself free from any thought or feeling that tells you—you can't. Because YOU CAN. We are excited to be your coaches throughout these pages, and together we will make your dreams a reality.

Living Your Fired Up Life

With a fired up mindset, you are living in the present and are clear about your intentions. You have no time for worry because you are busy doing what you love to do. You are thinking in terms of possibilities and solutions, so there is no room for self-pity or doubt. Things that in the past seemed difficult or even impossible suddenly become natural and fun. Since excessive negative stress is no longer a part of your life, your energy level is consistently high. You realize that what you feel and think is exactly what you attract.

Living a totally fired up life is something you create within yourself. You know that life is not a dress rehearsal and that each moment is the real thing. As a fired up person, you appreciate your problems because they provide an opportunity for growth.

Fired up people know this truth:
You will never feel good tomorrow until you feel good now.
You will never stop procrastinating until you take action now.
You will never be clear about what you really want until you start becoming clear now.

Please be aware that as you read this book, we know you are totally capable and …

We Totally Believe In You!

Who Do You Think You Are?

We gravitate toward our most dominant thoughts. If your thoughts are about your problems and frustrations, more of those will appear. Let's focus now on your strengths so you can attract more good thoughts. Write in the spaces below fifteen positive qualities that you possess. Forget about modesty; just let the good stuff roll.

Memory Joggers

1._____

Kind

2._____

Understanding

Optimistic

3._____

Organized

Persistent

4._____

Patient

Responsible

5._____

Open-minded

Happy

6._____

Adventurous

Healthy

7._____

Loving

Fearless

8._____

Bold

Honest

9._____

Motivated

Sense of humor

10._____

Trusting

Generous

11._____

12._____

13._____

14._____

15._____

Cooperative
Smart
Good parent
Achiever
Good planner
Goal setter
Highly energetic
Good listener

"If you follow your bliss … doors will open for you that wouldn't have opened for anyone else."—Joseph Campbell

What Do You Really Want?

Who says you can't have it, don't deserve it, or are not qualified for it? Let's clear the air right now. You have permission to live your life exactly the way you want to live it. The key is to become clear on what you really want. When you are clear, opportunities present themselves. Do you want love, wealth, energy, health, fun, spiritual connection, adventure, peace, family, or personal growth? Do you want it all? Answer the following questions to gain clarity.

1. What do I really, really want for my life right now?

_____

_____

_____

_____

_____

_____

2. How will I feel when it all comes to be?

_____

_____

_____

_____

_____

3. How will I feel if none of it comes to be?

_____

_____

_____

_____

_____

_____

Not sure what you really, really want? Give it a little time. As you continue to explore these secrets, what you want will surface and you will be on your way.

What Are My Limits?

"*Interestingly, koi, when put in a fish bowl, will only grow up to three inches. When this same fish is placed in a large tank, it will grow to about nine inches long. In a pond, koi can reach lengths of eighteen inches. Amazingly, when placed in a lake, koi can grow to three feet long. The metaphor is obvious. You are limited by how you see the world.*"

—Vince Poscente
www.vinceposcente.com

Take another look at yourself. How limited are you really?

Secret Number One

Activate the Law of Attraction

You attract to your life what you focus on whether you want it or not. What you focus on with feeling becomes your reality.

- Focus on how tired you are and the more tired you become. Instead, focus on having high energy and enthusiasm.

- Focus on your lack of money and the more money you lack. Instead, focus on abundance.

- Focus on your stress and the more stress you feel. Instead, focus on being calm and relaxed.

"Whatever is going on in your mind is what you are attracting."
—excerpt from *The Secret*

It's No Longer a Secret

Now that *The Secret* is out, there is never a reason to continue to live an unfulfilled life. *The Secret* is one of the most motivating books ever created. This simple, yet powerful book has received thumbs up from Oprah Winfrey, as well as business leaders and educators from around the globe.

The principle of *The Secret* is this: Like attracts like; it's the power of attraction. For every thought and feeling that you have, you will attract the same in your life. When you feel angry and unhappy, you attract more anger and unhappiness. When you focus on lack, you attract more lack.

How about attracting the good stuff? Remember a time when you felt wonderful? You awoke in the morning filled with endless energy. In your mind was a clear picture of what you wanted for your life. You couldn't wait to greet the world. What happened? Your world met you with the same positive energy. You were in the zone, attracting what you wanted.

Andrew had heard that we help many people to attract what they want in their lives. He told us he watched *The Secret* and it made sense, but it didn't seem to work for him. He said, "I did what *The Secret* suggested. I created a mental picture of what I wanted. I could see myself receiving a promotion to vice president. I visualized my new spacious office and my new secretary. I heard my co-workers congratulate me and I felt great. So here I am. After four months I still have no promotion."

We reminded Andrew that *The Secret* helps you attract whatever you want and focus on with feeling. We asked Andrew what thoughts he had about his company when he was home. "Well," he said, "I must admit that I have been very negative. I told my wife that my co-workers are always back stabbing and complaining, and I'm not sure I want to work in that type of atmosphere."

The power of attraction was working. Andrew's strong negative pictures and feelings about the company were stronger than his vision of success. He was attracting what he didn't want. He then began sending out a more positive vibration by thinking only about his intention. He visualized and felt his dream as if it were already his. The reactions of others started to change. He is now certain that a promotion is forthcoming.

Decide what you want. Create a mental picture of having and enjoying your goal. Think of it with deep positive feelings. Avoid any thought of what you don't want. Your **inspired actions** will bring you success. You will be on a path to the life you really want.

"When you are in a state of joy, happiness, or appreciation, you are attracting more of that into your life. What you focus on expands."—Esther Hicks

Activate the Law of Attraction

To attract more of what you want in your life, focus on what you are grateful for in this moment. Write down your thoughts.

_____

_____

_____

_____

_____

_____

_____

_____

_____

_____

_____

The Law of Attraction will continue to provide you with what you want or with what you don't want, depending on what you are focusing on with feeling. So, think the good thoughts, and when you are inspired to act, act immediately.

Secret Number Two

What's Working?

We move in the direction of our
most dominant thoughts.

"If 98 percent of your life is working and you place 100 percent of your attention on the two percent that isn't working, in that moment 100 percent of your life is not working. If 98 percent of your life isn't working and you place 100 percent of your attention on the two percent that is, in that moment 100 percent of your life is working."—Author Unknown

(Read again)

Choose to focus only on what's working.
Positive results will begin to multiply themselves.

"The inner speech, your thoughts, can cause you to be rich or poor, loved or unloved, happy or not happy, attractive or unattractive, powerful or weak."
—James Allen

What's Working?

In Secret Number One we focused on The Law of Attraction. We illustrated how Andrew's negative thoughts and feelings were stronger than his vision of success, and he received what he didn't want.

What do you say when you talk to yourself? "There is no way I can do this, but I'll make one more attempt." "Must be nice, but I could never do that." "If I could only get unstuck." Or are you a person who practices positive self talk? "I have faced tough situations before and I know I can make this happen." "I have the confidence and skills necessary to help me succeed."

You can use your powerful imagination to create a vision of what you want in your life. Your mind believes what you tell it repeatedly with feeling. Here's an example: Imagine picking up a large, ripe lemon. You slice it open and let the juices flow out. You smell the tangy fruit. Now you bite into the lemon and let the imaginary juice squirt into your mouth. Is your mouth watering? Do your lips pucker? Can you actually taste the lemon?

Albert Einstein said, *"Imagination is more important than knowledge. Knowledge is limited. Imagination encircles the world."*

Jack became a client of ours because he was coming up short when trying to reach his career goals. He had a strong desire to be a successful stockbroker. He started his career with enthusiasm, but soon ran out of gas when he found himself a below average producer. He loved golf and began each season with high expectations, but he never seemed to improve his game.

We asked Jack to write down what he focused on and what he said to himself when he was working toward his goals. As you can imagine, his thoughts were less than positive. "I guess I'm not meant to be a stockbroker." "What is wrong with me?" "It's not my fault." "If only I were stronger and smarter." We then asked Jack to think about and write down what was working in each area of his life. Jack made a commitment to focus on these new thoughts with positive feelings every day for the next ten days.

Was it easy for Jack? Not at first. Did things change for the better? Yes! Was it instant and like magic? No! It was a gradual process, but Jack soon had a new momentum and to him it seemed like magic. He was becoming free from his old, self-defeating thoughts. He looked better. He felt better. He was better. Soon Jack had one word for how he felt about his life. Terrific! New opportunities started opening for him. He was attracting what he really wanted. He said, "The stronger my positive feelings become, the more of what I want seems to show up. I feel like a magnet."

Ask yourself this: What in my life is not quite the way I want it to be? Am I focusing on that? Or am I focusing on what's working? Whatever you are focusing on will begin to manifest in your life. Choose to focus on what's working and how you want your world to be. You will then be creating your own magic.

"You are searching for the magic key that will unlock the door to the source of power, and yet you have the key in your own hands, and you may use it the moment you learn to control your thoughts."—Napoleon Hill

What's Working in My Life?

When you choose to focus on what's working in your life, what you focus on expands. Answer the following questions:

What's working in my business? _____
_____

What's working in my home life? _____
_____

What's working in my social life? _____
_____

What's working with my health? _____
_____

What's working with my finances? _____
_____

What's working with my relationships? _____
_____

Secret Number Three

Ask Your Way to Success

Ask questions that will move you out of your comfort zone toward what you really want.

Ask yourself:

What will happen if I keep doing what I have been doing?

How can I be even more effective?

Who can help me make this happen?

Ask others:

How did you create your success?

What do I need to learn to be successful?

Will you help me?

Asking Good Questions is the Answer

Ask Your Way to Success

"I keep six honest serving-men,
They taught me all I knew;
Their names are What and Why and When
And How and Where and Who."—Rudyard Kipling

People who seem to have everything they want have the habit of asking questions. The questions they ask are designed to help them acquire exactly what they want and need.

Children are masters of asking. Can I have this? Can I have that? Will you help me with this? Why can't I do that?

Why have so many adults lost this ability to ask? Here's the answer: We are afraid of the "R" word, which is rejection. We try everything possible to avoid rejection. So what if someone says no to your request? Are you any worse off than before you asked? Actually, you are in the same situation as before and perhaps you learned something new about yourself. The most important lesson you can learn is that avoiding asking for what you want makes no sense.

A joke from Jack Canfield's book, *The Aladdin Factor: "Why does it take a million sperm cells to fertilize one egg? Because the stubborn little guys won't stop and ask for directions!"*

Why do some people seem to have almost everything they want in life? This answer will not surprise you. THEY ASK! They don't allow the "R" word to get in their way. They keep asking until they get the answers that they want. They ask for directions. They ask for ideas. They ask how. They ask when. They ask where. They ask why. Are you thinking, if asking is the key, why are there so many people who never come close to getting exactly what they want?

The answer is this: It's important to know how to ask.

In this book we talk a lot about attracting what we want. The Law of Attraction says that you will attract into your life what you want or what you don't want, depending on your focus.

When you ask for what you want, be sure to ask for **what you want,** not for what you don't want. For example, if your teenager is yelling and demanding something and you ask him to stop yelling, your focus is still on the yelling. If you ask him to speak in a more respectful tone, you're asking for what you really want.

Be clear and specific. Make sure there is no fuzzy thinking when you ask. Think about what you want and what you need.

Remember, there is someone who knows exactly how you can get what you want. Most successful people who have attained what you want will be happy to share this information with you. All you have to do is ask.

"You create your opportunities by asking for them."—Shakti Gawain

Asking is the Key to Knowing and Getting

If you don't know how to get from where you are to where you want to be, it may be because you didn't ask. Perhaps you asked the wrong question or the wrong person, or you asked the question in the wrong way.

If you don't ask, you don't get. Do you have a goal that you really want, but you don't have a clue how to get it? Ask yourself the following questions:

Who has it now? _____

When will I contact this person?_____

What questions will I ask? _____

_____

_____

_____

_____

_____

_____

_____

_____

_____

_____

_____

Secret Number Four

Listen—Listen—Listen

"Most of the successful people I've known are the ones who do more listening than talking."—Bernard Baruch

"A good listener is not only popular everywhere, but after a while he gets to know something."—Wilson Mizner

"The wise old owl lived in an oak;
The more he saw the less he spoke;
The less he spoke the more he heard;
Why can't we all be like that old bird?"
—Author Unknown

Listen—Listen—Listen

Has this ever happened to you? You meet a friend from work who has an idea he would like you to hear. As he explains his idea, you wish he would hurry so you could share *your* idea. You become uneasy and your friend senses your disinterest. What happened to the conversation?

The skill of being a good listener can be the determining factor for your success in business as well as in personal relationships.

Kyle was a hard-working salesperson. In spite of this, he was unable to earn the income he wanted. He said, "I talk to hundreds of prospects, and yet I am unable to make many sales." He was beginning to think he wasn't cut out for this business. Kyle needed to know why his efforts were not paying off. He hired us to help him figure out what was wrong.

We asked Kyle about his conversations with potential buyers. "How do you discover what your prospects want?" "What questions do you ask?" "Who is doing most of the talking?" Kyle soon realized that because he was so eager to make a sale, he asked few questions and did most of the talking. He wasn't listening, even when his prospects gave him buying signals.

This realization was life changing for Kyle. He began to really listen. He would continue to listen until he knew exactly what his prospect wanted and why. His success amazed himself and his sales manager. One of his buyers actually complimented him for being an excellent conversationalist, even though Kyle spent ninety percent of his time just listening.

Yes, being a good listener is vital and it requires patience. Take time to listen to your children, wife, husband, friends, business associates, and customers. When listening becomes your priority, it pays huge dividends.

Some DO'S for effective listening:

DO ... Listen without judging.
This will generate an atmosphere of trust with the other person.

DO ... Avoid interrupting people.
Before you speak, make sure the other person has finished talking.

DO ... Be aware of body language.
The person's gestures, tone of voice, body posture, and facial expressions may say more than words.

DO ... Look at the person speaking to you.
Make eye contact so the speaker feels he or she has your total attention.

DO ... Ask questions.
The other person will know you are interested in the conversation.

It's rare to find people who will take the time to really listen to what others say. When you do this, you will be listening your way to success.

"The most basic of all human needs is the need to understand and be understood. The best way to understand people is to listen to them."
—Ralph G. Nichols

Here's your challenge:

Choose a friend. It could even be your wife or husband. Ask that person about an event in his or her life that you know a little about, but not the entire picture. Show sincere interest in what you are hearing. Your goal is to go for clarity. Ask and listen. Some possible questions to ask:

When did this take place?
Who was involved?
How did you make it happen?
Why did you choose to do it?
How did you feel?
What was the outcome?

The key to being a good listener is to practice, practice, practice. When you listen, you will be amazed at what you will discover about the other person, even if it is someone you think you know well.

Secret Number Five

Fear is Not to be Feared

Are you avoiding something? Is it because of fear?

Fear is merely a reaction to a possible outcome. After you take action, fear disappears. Eliminating fear can be this simple. If fear is stopping you from taking action, follow the advice of Eleanor Roosevelt, who said,

"Do the thing you fear the most and the death of fear is certain."

"Come to the edge," he said.
They said, "We are afraid."
"Come to the edge," he said.
They came.
He pushed them....
And they flew.
—Guillaume Apollinaire

The Fear Factor

What is stopping you from going all out for the life you really want? Take a few moments and think about this question. You are aware that this present moment is not a dress rehearsal. You know this is it. This is your life. You know that NOW is the only time you will ever have. Yet you stop yourself because of a voice in your head that says, "What if I fail? What will others think?"

Our coaching clients receive a "wake up call" when they realize that they are allowing these fearful thoughts to stop them from living their dreams. They take a long hard look at what they have been avoiding.

Fear has no power unless you allow it to enter your mind. Is it fear of failure? Fear of success? Fear of change? Fear of certain people? Fear of rejection? Fear has been defined as **F**alse **E**vidence **A**ppearing **R**eal. The good news is this: Fear is not real. It's only a feeling. It's a feeling that something bad is going to happen instead of something good.

> **What if** I make that call and I'm rejected?
> **What if** I apply for that position and I don't get it?
> **What if** I succeed and I can't handle the responsibilities?
> **What if** I propose marriage and I get a big "No"?
> What if? What if? What if?

You can let that feeling go. You can release it.

Ask yourself this question instead: What if I succeed and my plans work out just the way I want? So, in the past I had a few failures. So what? Be aware of the words of Elbert Hubbard: *"Constant effort and frequent mistakes are the stepping stones of genius."*

Keep moving toward what you want. Let go of your fear. It will crumble because of your clear intention and you will grow in confidence and courage. You will then begin to witness the life you have been dreaming about. You will actually be living it.

As George Bernard Shaw said, *"People are always blaming their circumstances for what they are. I don't believe in circumstances. The people who get on in this world are the people who get up and look for the circumstances they want and, if they can't find them, make them."*

Repeat these words until they become a natural part of your self talk:

"Fear is just an illusion."

"Here's an uncomfortable bit of information:
People give up because they are scared."—Anonymous

Think of a time when you wanted something that seemed almost impossible. You wanted it intensely and somehow you crashed through your fear and made it happen.

Describe the situation: _____

_____

_____

_____

_____

How did you want it to be? _____

_____

_____

_____

_____

What roadblocks did you encounter? _____

_____

_____

_____

_____

What did you do to make it happen your way?_____

_____

_____

_____

_____

What thoughts did you focus on?

_____

_____

_____

_____

_____

What qualities did you display that made it happen?
(Positive attitude? Determination? Understanding? Enthusiasm? Love?)

_____

_____

_____

_____

_____

You can make what seems impossible—possible!

Secret Number Six

Let's Pretend

Don't wait for success any longer.
BE the person you want to be NOW!

Do you need more enthusiasm?
Act enthusiastic and you'll be enthusiastic.

Do you feel a little down and uninspired?
Remember the song, "Pretend you're happy when you're blue."

Want more prosperity?
Act prosperous and opportunities for prosperity will appear.

Want to be liked and have more friends?
Act friendlier and friends will show up.

"You can't build a reputation on what you are going to do."
—Henry Ford

Let's Pretend

Dr. Maxwell Maltz, the author of the remarkable book *Psycho-Cybernetics*, says the mind cannot tell the difference between an action that is real and one that is vividly imagined. This is not just a theory to have fun thinking about; it is a real world skill that will accelerate your progress toward what you consider success. It will help you in every situation.

Picture this: You are scheduled to be a presenter to a group of one hundred executives. Your audience will have just finished dinner and drinks, and are probably in a festive mood or are sleepy. Since you have had little public speaking experience, your attitude is less than positive. Simply thinking of the event brings on sweaty palms, dry mouth, tense muscles, and shallow breathing. You ask yourself, "Why should these people listen to me?" "How can I get their positive attention?" "HELP! I need a coach to get me through this."

The Coach's Suggestions:
Pretend you are totally fearless.
Pretend you have exactly what your audience wants to hear.
Pretend you speak to crowds like this frequently.
Pretend you speak from your heart and don't need notes.
Pretend you own the company.

The time has arrived. You hear your introduction. Your heart skips a beat as you walk to the microphone. Your fear has turned to excitement and you feel as if you own the world.

Golfer Tiger Woods, as well as professionals in every sport, imagine success before they perform. Pretending is used by successful salespeople, managers, parents, and people in all walks of life.

Do this to gain confidence:

Find a quiet place where you can be alone. Close your eyes. Take deep breaths and slowly exhale. Feel the stress leave your body. Now focus on the situation you must meet with confidence. Tell yourself that you are confident and have the ability to do it successfully. Imagine going through the process and seeing successful results. Now open your eyes and smile. You are ready for the real thing. You have just experienced it successfully in your mind!

"Formulate and stamp indelibly on your mind a mental picture of yourself as succeeding. Hold this picture tenaciously. Never permit it to fade. Your mind will seek to develop the picture and make it real."—Norman Vincent Peale

Think of a challenge coming your way that you want to handle successfully. Pretend that you have already met the challenge. Write down your vision of this successful experience in vivid detail.

_____

_____

_____

_____

_____

_____

_____

_____

_____

_____

_____

_____

_____

Be sure to replay in your mind this vision prior to the actual event taking place. This will ensure your success!

Secret Number Seven

Happiness is the Way

As you move toward your goals and dreams ask yourself:

Am I enjoying the journey?

It's only the journey that matters. Even when your goal is attained, you are still on the journey. This day, this hour, this moment is where life takes place. Surrender to it and enjoy its riches.

"Yesterday's the past and tomorrow's the future. Today is a gift, which is why they call it the present."—Deepak Chopra

Happiness is the Way!

Are you looking for happiness in all the wrong places? "If I could just get the world to be the way I want it to be; then I'd be happy." "Look at that beautiful Lexus. If I owned that car, I'd really be happy." "If I could have his job, my life would be totally happy." "If my wife/husband would only change, then happiness would finally be mine."

What's the misconception? It's that things or people will make you happy. How can I get to them or find them? Where is happiness?

Jackie, a thirty-two-year-old successful executive living in New York, seemed to have everything. She had a great job, a wonderful family, and all the trappings of success, yet she felt something was missing. She told us, "I am searching for something that will make me happy."

When she hired us, she asked one question: "What is the secret to being happy?" We explained to her that the secret to happiness is simply this: There is no secret. That answer, of course, frustrated her even more.

Jackie was very goal-oriented. She was constantly trying to attain something in the future that she felt would make her life more complete. After two coaching sessions, she had an "aha" moment. She said, "I've been totally waiting to live in the future so I could never be happy with my life right now."

Jackie began to focus on her present moment blessings. She soon realized that her happiness is here and now and not over there somewhere. Over there could mean five minutes, sixty minutes, or five years into the future. Yes, it's wise to have future goals, as long as they do not drag you into the future. You can't live there. Tomorrow never comes.

In the words of Ralph Waldo Emerson, *"The foolish man seeks happiness in the distance; the wise man grows it under his feet."*

Remember, happiness is a feeling. If what you are doing or thinking in this moment does not produce a feeling of well being, gently let that feeling go. Immerse yourself into what you love doing and savor the good feelings you receive. When you do this, not only will you feel great, but also the success you want will find you. You are totally in charge of your life and your life exists only in the present moment.

"The happiest people surround themselves with family and friends, don't care about keeping up with the people next door, lose themselves in daily activities and, most important, forgive easily."
—Quoted in *USA Today* from Authentic Happiness

"Act happy, feel happy, be happy, without a reason in the world. Then you can love, and do what you will."—Dan Millman

What will really make you happy?
When I get that job, then I'll be happy. (Oops, my boss is a real jerk.)
When I live in Florida, then I'll be happy. (Oh no, high humidity.)
When I find a mate, then I'll be happy. (What a slob he became.)
When I'm rich, then I'll be happy. (Everyone now wants a handout.)
When I lose weight, then I'll be happy. (I lost it and gained it all back.)

Happiness is not out there somewhere. Happiness is the journey. You can choose the journey.

I choose to be happy on the job because:

_____

_____

_____

I choose to be happy at home because:

_____

_____

_____

I choose to be happy in my community because:

_____

_____

_____

I choose to be happy by myself because:

_____

_____

_____

Secret Number Eight

Ignite Your Sense of Humor

You will reduce your stress.
You will be happier and healthier.
You will be even more productive.

"Laughter is the shortest distance between two people."—Victor Borge

"Among those whom I like or admire, I can find no common denominator, but among those whom I love, I can; all of them make me laugh."—W. H. Auden

"Seven days without laughter makes one weak."—Mort Walker

"Laughter gives us distance. It allows us to step back from an event, deal with it, and then move on."—Bob Newhart

"For every sixty seconds of anger you lose one minute of happiness."
—Ralph Waldo Emerson

Laugh Yourself Happy, Healthy, and Successful

Woody Allen said, *"Laughter is like the human body wagging its tail."*

It's been said that a good belly laugh is internal jogging. When you laugh, how is your energy level? When you laugh, how stressed do you feel? When you laugh and are happy, how do other people react to you?

We have long known that the ability to laugh is helpful to those coping with a major illness and the stress of life's problems. Researchers are now saying laughter can do a lot more; it can bring balance to all the components of the immune system, which help us fight off diseases. People who laugh often earn more, play more, and live longer.

During one of our group coaching sessions, we noticed that the chemistry among the participants was just not right. We were doing what had always worked, but this time the spark of fun was missing. We, the coaches, immediately made fun of ourselves for being so serious. Laughter began to take over. Everyone became more spontaneous. As a result, the participants received greater results. They were motivated to put their new strategies and attitudes into action.

It's no joke. Laughter is important. Laugh at your successes. Laugh at your failures. Most importantly, laugh at yourself.

To put more laughter into your life:

1. Figure out what makes you laugh, and then laugh. Read about laughing, or watch somebody else laughing. Then laugh often.

2. Surround yourself with funny people.

3. Develop your own sense of humor. Maybe even take a class to learn how to be a better comic, or at least a better joke teller at the next party.

4. Use humor frequently, as long as it's not at someone else's expense!

Researchers estimate that laughing 100 times is equal to 10 minutes on the rowing machine or 15 minutes on an exercise bike. Laughing can be a total body workout! Blood pressure is lowered. There is an increase in vascular blood flow and in oxygenation of the blood, which further assists healing. Laughter also gives your diaphragm and abdominal, respiratory, facial, leg, and back muscles a workout. That's why you often feel exhausted after a long bout of laughter—you've just had an aerobic workout!   —*Prevention Magazine*

"At the height of laughter, the universe is flung into a kaleidoscope of new possibilities."—Jean Houston

Funny is Good

Look for the humor in all the circumstances in your life. If you are not used to having a good laugh, go to a quiet place where you can be alone and then fake it until you make it. Yes, just laugh!

What makes you laugh anyway?

_____
_____
_____
_____
_____
_____
_____
_____

Always look for humor. It will make the low points of your life seem higher and the high points even higher!

Secret Number Nine

Persistence Wins

Include on your "TO-DO" list only those things that you intend to totally complete.

When you take persistent action:
You will develop an "I Can Attitude"
Your obstacles will crumble before you
You will be in charge of your life

"Persist and persevere, and you will find that most things are attainable."
—Lord Chesterfield

Persistence Wins

So you think the speed of light is fast. How about the speed of life? It's like the blink of an eye. Where did the time go? Remember all those plans and all those dreams? Is it ever too late to do what you want to do? Many of our coaching clients say no, absolutely not. A retired stockbroker took up piano at the age of seventy-eight. A sixty-five-year-old school teacher lost thirty pounds. She looks and feels great. An eighty-three-year-old businessman has a new wife and a new life. There's a never-ending buffet of options waiting for you. Just look around.

Take a moment now and do some pretending. In your imagination, think of one unfulfilled dream you once had. Think of something you wanted to be or do and for some reason your life took a different turn. What do you see? What do you hear? How does it make you feel? Remember the old saying, "Life begins at forty?" Life also begins at fifty, sixty, seventy, and eighty. Life begins whenever you choose to invent yourself along the way and live the life of your dreams.

Thomas Edison knew the power of persistence when he said, *"I have not failed. I've just found 10,000 ways that won't work."*

What small step can you now take to move toward what you really want?

As you begin taking persistent action your enthusiasm will grow, you will have a new momentum, and you will feel better physically. No, you won't be twenty-one again, but you could feel like it. You may not become a professional golf star, but you will knock some strokes off your game. You may not run a marathon, but you could be walking five miles a day. You may not become a speed-reader, but you could start reading some of the classics you have been thinking about for years.

Can you make it happen? Of course you can. Take a moment and brainstorm your personal and business strengths. Look at how many positive things you have going for you. Take a look at the qualities that made you successful in the past. These are the same qualities you have now. At any age you only use a small fraction of your potential. Go ahead and dare to do and be what you **really** want. Dare to be happy!

"That which we persist in doing becomes easier, not that the nature of the task has changed, but our ability to do has increased."—Ralph Waldo Emerson

Trust This Wisdom and Succeed

*"To get through the hardest journey we need take only one step at a time, but we must **KEEP ON STEPPING**."*—Chinese Proverb

*"**KEEP ON GOING**, and the chances are that you will stumble on something, perhaps when you are least expecting it. I never heard of anyone ever stumbling on something sitting down."*—Charles F. Kettering

*"**KEEP ON SOWING YOUR SEED,** for you never know which will grow. Perhaps it all will."*—Albert Einstein

Think of three goals that require your persistence. Write them in the blank spaces below and repeat the sentences to yourself throughout the day.

Example: I will persist (<u>in making ten sales calls a day</u>) until I succeed!

I will persist_____ until I succeed!

I will persist_____ until I succeed!

I will persist _____until I succeed!

Secret Number Ten

Danger—Hesitation Ahead

Are you waiting for things to be
just right before you take action?

What if you knew you could not fail?
What would you do? Where would you go?

According to the law of aerodynamics, the bumblebee can't fly.
However, the bumblebee does not know this law and flies effortlessly.

"If you wait until all the lights are 'green' before you leave home,
you'll never get started on your trip to the top."—Zig Ziglar

Mission Impossible? Not!

When a problem appears, ask yourself, "What are the possibilities?"
When you hit a roadblock, ask yourself, "What are the possibilities?"
When you get a new idea, ask yourself, "What are the possibilities?"
You will be in an upward spiral toward what you want in your life.

Ask yourself again, "What do I really, really, REALLY want?" Feel the feeling of having it now. When you are inspired to take action, don't hesitate. Take it immediately. This is how you attract what you want. NOW is the best time to put it into action.

Keep in mind this great poem by Edgar A. Guest:

"There are thousands to tell you it cannot be done,
There are thousands to prophesy failure;
There are thousands to point out to you, one by one,
The dangers that wait to assail you.
But just buckle in with a bit of a grin,
Just take off your coat and go to it;
Just start to sing as you tackle the thing
That 'cannot be done' and you'll do it."

Remember a time when you had a really great idea? You were excited and couldn't wait to look further into the possibilities. You ran the idea past well-meaning friends. Remember their responses? "You have got to be kidding." "No way will that work." "Silly idea; it's never been done before." "Be realistic." And you said to yourself, "I guess this idea is just a pipe dream, and they are probably right." The idea faded away. Sometime later, you had a rude awakening. You opened the newspaper and saw an article about someone who was putting into action the very idea you had discarded. Your idea became successful for someone else.

When you remain focused on the possibilities and have a clear vision of the result you want, the actions to take will appear. The desired outcome can and will be yours. Mission impossible? Not!

If what you want is so special, why don't you have it now? What negative input have you been listening to?

Who didn't listen to the naysayers? Thomas Edison didn't listen when he was told that the phonograph had no commercial value. John F. Kennedy didn't listen when he was told by experts that going to the moon was impossible. Sir Roger Bannister didn't listen when he was told that running a four-minute mile was a physical impossibility. Remember the time you didn't listen and went on to accomplish what you wanted? Now is your time to act.

"Upon the plains of hesitation lie the bones of countless millions who, on the verge of victory, lay down to rest and resting they died. (It's not over till it's over.)"
—Adlai E. Stevenson

Hesitation Self Talk

"I'm not sure my idea will be accepted."
"What if I didn't do enough research?"
"Do I really want to expend the necessary energy?"
"If I fail they will laugh."
"I'm not sure I'm totally ready."
"Is this really what I want?"

My positive self talk is this:

_____
_____
_____
_____

   Yes! What you want is possible! No one is keeping score; this gives you freedom. Keep moving toward your dream and readjust as you go.
Do not allow yourself or others to talk you out of what you want.

Secret Number Eleven

Live the Right Dream for You

When you think about your dream do you
sometimes say to yourself

"I Wish I Woulda."
"I Think I Coulda."
"I Know I Shoulda."

Your dream may seem out of reach, but not for long if you start now!

"It's never too late to be what you might have been."
—George Eliot

"When a dream takes hold of you, what can you do? You can run with it, let it run your life, or let it go and think for the rest of your life about what might have been."—Patch Adams

Live the Right Dream for You

Does your dream life still excite you? Are you staying on that track because you think it's what you "should" do? After all, you planned for it, made investments of time and money in it, took risks, and told everyone about it. So, do you feel guilty if it's no longer what you really want? Do you wonder what other people will think if you go in an entirely new direction?

During our first coaching session with Adam, he said he felt embarrassed. After working hard and sacrificing for years to build his business, he was no longer excited about his career. He was living what he thought was to be his dream life, operating his own advertising agency. He had contracts with large organizations and his business was quite successful. However, his passion was gone. The joy was dulled. He no longer looked forward to going to work.

Through coaching, Adam realized that as time goes by, our dreams for our life can change. He also realized that other people had their own concerns and were not making judgments about him. Adam was now free to think about new careers that would stir his passion. His excitement about his future returned.

Are you trapped by your old dreams? Ask yourself these questions to determine if the life you are living is really what you want:

1. Do I awaken each morning with a passion for the day?

2. Throughout the day do I appreciate the lows as well as the highs?

3. At the end of the day do I have a joyful tiredness that says, "I would love what I'm doing, even if I were doing it for free."

If you are not certain that what you do is really what you want, fine-tune it, expand it, or simply drop it if it doesn't inspire you any longer. Choose your new dream. Whose life is it anyway?

Doing what you love is the cornerstone of having abundance in your life."
—Dr. Wayne Dyer

There's an old saying, *"If you haven't gotta dream, how ya gonna make that dream come true?"*

It's time to write down again what you really, really want. Update it or change it completely. Make sure it's your dream and not somebody else's.

_____

_____

_____

_____

_____

_____

_____

_____

_____

_____

_____

_____

_____

Hold on to this vision until it becomes a reality.

Secret Number Twelve

Sharpen Your People Skills

Look at the challenges in your life.
Do most of those have to do with other people?

The secret for dealing effectively with others is to
see things from their point of view without judgment.

"The only way to have a friend is to be one."—Ralph Waldo Emerson

Sharpen Your People Skills

People are everywhere. Wherever you go, there they are. Even when you think you would like to avoid them, they show up. The way you relate to others can be the key to your success and happiness, or the reason for your stress and unhappiness.

How can you fine-tune your people skills so they become a wonderful asset to your success? There is a way. First, it's not memorizing a list of rules and trying to use them on others. It's about understanding basic principles that will help you to see things from the other person's point of view.

A large firm that offers plenty of opportunities for growth employs our client Gary. After working hard for three years, Gary was still in the same position as he had been in since he was hired. He needed his manager's approval and recommendation for a promotion. We asked Gary how he felt about Mr. Wilson, his manager. Gary said, "This man has a deaf ear to everything I suggest. There's something about him I just don't like." Gary went on to describe what he considered were Mr. Wilson's negative qualities. "When I try to tell him how valuable I can be to the company, he seems to brush it off as unimportant."

We asked Gary how well he knew Mr. Wilson on a personal level. Gary admitted that he knew almost nothing about him. Gary decided that it was time to turn that around, so he scheduled an appointment to talk with Mr. Wilson. It turned out that they had several interests in common. They both enjoyed scuba diving and deep-sea fishing. A friendship developed and numerous conversations followed.

After a period of time, Gary received a call from the company president. Gary was offered a much better position based on Mr. Wilson's recommendation.

This promotion did not take place simply because Gary was friendly. His sincere friendliness opened the door to communication. Mr. Wilson no longer had a deaf ear to Gary's ideas.

Don't expect what you don't expect. The key is being sincere. Have you ever experienced that the harder you tried to be a friend, the farther away that person drifted? Perhaps there was something about the person that bothered you or made you feel uncomfortable. The other person will always, at some level, pick up your true feelings. Change your thinking about the person and change your results.

"Constant kindness can accomplish much. As the sun makes ice melt, kindness causes misunderstanding, mistrust and hostility to evaporate."
—Albert Schweitzer

Don't Criticize—Harmonize

With whom do you want to have a better relationship?

_____

What action will you take?

_____
_____
_____

Four fundamental people skills that will change your life for the better:

1. Mind off judgment. Don't criticize!
2. Mind on appreciation. Pay sincere compliments.
3. Show genuine interest in other people.
4. Smile from the inside.

Don't let the simplicity of these ideas stop you from acting. They will produce results.

Secret Number Thirteen

Appreciation Makes the Difference

"The deepest principle of human nature is the craving to be appreciated."
—William James

When you show sincere appreciation:

People will see you as someone who really cares.

People will become more open to your ideas and suggestions.

People will feel better about themselves.

"Everyone has an invisible sign hanging from their neck saying please help me feel important."—Mary Kay Ash

Appreciation Makes the Difference

When you think about the problems and frustrations in your life, how many of those have to do with other people? "I would never be critical if he would just shape up." "I can't seem to get along with my boss." "He just doesn't get it." "We argue and argue and that's about it." "My ideas are never accepted." "I don't feel appreciated."

Rudy was frustrated with his teenage son, David. Whenever they were together there was a feeling of tension. Neither of them could relax. When Rudy scheduled coaching with us, he had just about given up. He had no clue how to develop harmony with his son. During our coaching sessions, the real cause of the problem emerged. With good intentions, Rudy was constantly critical of his son, telling David how he should correct whatever he was doing. So what happened? David reacted as you and I would react when we are constantly criticized. He showed resentment. He became angry and tried to defend his position. He talked back and placed blame on his parents.

What to do? We offered Rudy this exercise: For one week refrain from criticizing anyone or anything. If the need to criticize appears, think about what you like or admire about the person or situation.

This is not an easy exercise. Some of us would last only a few minutes. Rudy was ready to try anything. He was ready to go out on a limb and give it his best effort, even though he thought this might be an impossible task.

Was it simple? No. Rudy slipped up again and again, but he kept on going. He told us this. "David was in his room when I knocked on his door. When he answered, I noticed he was defensive immediately and was waiting for a critical remark." I said, "Hi, David. How was your day? How about a round of golf after dinner?" There was a lot of silence until David realized no critical remarks were coming. When Rudy noticed the positive results, he was amazed. He also felt guilty for letting this go on for so long. Needless to say, the father and son relationship improved.

Do you want more harmony in your relationships? Try taking your mind off of judgment. Ask yourself what you like or admire about your wife, husband, boss, son, or daughter. Now, instead of criticism, pay a sincere compliment. It could change your life as well as the lives of others.

Why not give it a go? No critical remarks for one week. Show appreciation for everything in your life. If you forget and revert to being the critic, don't beat yourself up. Start again from that point. It's worth the effort. This could be the most worthwhile exercise you have ever performed. Remember, the word with real power is appreciation.

"Flatter me, and I may not believe you. Criticize me, and I may not like you. Ignore me, and I may not forgive you. Show me appreciation, and I will never forget you."—William Arthur Ward

The Power of Honest and Sincere Appreciation

Do you ever get so caught up in what's urgent in your life that you walk right by your friends and associates without taking notice of them? Perhaps they deserved a compliment or a word of encouragement, which you only thought of later. As soon as you slow down and show appreciation, your world will change for the better.

Make a commitment to show sincere appreciation whenever you can. Your spouse and children are doing remarkable things. Your friends are doing remarkable things. The stranger sitting next to you in a meeting or on a plane is doing remarkable things. Show interest. Compliment them and positive sparks will fly.

These people need more appreciation from me:

Name: What I will say:

_____   _____

_____   _____

_____   _____

_____   _____

_____   _____

Secret Number Fourteen

Say Good-bye to Self-doubt

The next time self-doubt creeps in, instead of trying to figure it out, visualize a *"Doubt Delete Button"* in your mind. Hit the *"Doubt Delete Button"* and feel the subtle change in your attitude as doubt becomes weaker and weaker. With your new mental freedom, look at all the possibilities and take action. How much effort does this take?

How much effort did it take to put self-doubt in your mind? Would you rather have doubt or would you rather be free?

"Devote today to something so daring even you can't believe you're doing it."
—*Oprah Winfrey*

Say Good-bye to Self-doubt

Imagine yourself in this picture: I awaken in the morning with a broad smile on my face. I feel excited as I zip out of bed and prepare for my day. I picture in my mind the crystal clear details of the life I intend to create for myself. I sense that my positive expectation is contagious as the people in my life become in tune with my ideas. I move effortlessly from one task to another, feeling certain that this will be the best day of my life.

How can you capture this feeling and make it a constant part of your life every day? You may be thinking, *"Sure sounds good, but you don't realize that I struggle with indecision. My mind constantly goes back to times when I failed. I feel anxious when I go into unfamiliar situations. I know what I want, but I just don't believe that I can have it, so I fail to act."*

The good life comes in "Cans." You can if you think you can. However, when self-doubt creeps in, the more you think about it, the stronger it becomes.

Self-doubt comes from one place only. It comes from your real and imagined memories. You remember when you were rejected. You tried something and failed. You were criticized unjustly.

Physicists have proven that everything is energy. You can direct your energy to ignore those memories or erase the feelings they produce. You can even rewrite your negative memories using your imagination.

Do this simple exercise to rid yourself of doubt. It works like magic for many of our coaching clients. If you visualize these pictures consistently for at least twenty-one days, you will begin to move forward with confidence and motivation.

Courageous: Think of a time when you acted courageously. Visualize the picture.

Confident: Think of a time when you acted with confidence in a new situation. Visualize the picture.

Positive: Think of a time when you were positive when others were negative. Visualize the picture.

Energetic: Think of a time when you had high energy and others were tired. Visualize the picture.

Next, say the following familiar sentence to yourself every day:

"Today is the best day of my life and tomorrow will be even better."

Then, for the next thirty seconds, focus on the pictures that appear in your imagination. The result will be increased momentum.

"You become what you think about all day long."
—Ralph Waldo Emerson

When you were small you couldn't walk. You tried to walk and you fell down. You didn't say, "I know I'll never walk." You fell down again and again. Eventually, you got up and took one step and then another. And there you were ... a walker.

Take Baby Steps to Total Confidence

Think about what you are avoiding because you doubt that you can. Then choose the baby step you will take to move forward. Write both down.

I doubt that I can: Baby step I will take:

_____   _____

_____   _____

_____   _____

_____   _____

_____   _____

You are in charge of you and you always have been.

Secret Number Fifteen

Live for the Fun of It

The best part of having fun is that you really don't need a reason to do it. Having fun puts a twinkle in your eye. You will think more clearly. You will reduce your stress level. You will be happier. You will be more fun to be around. You will be more creative.

We don't have space to list the two million additional reasons to have fun.

YOU GET THE IDEA!

"You don't stop having fun because you grow old.
You grow old because you stop having fun."—Anonymous

Living for the Fun of It!

At the grocery store, the checker asked a child, "Is school fun?" "Sure," the little girl replied enthusiastically. She was asked what plans she had for summer vacation. "I don't have plans," the girl answered. "I'm a kid. I just have fun."

To a child, life is an adventure. Children are curious about everything. They live in the moment, even within the structure adults place on them. They fall down, skin their knees, cry, get up, laugh, and move on to the next fun thing. Children are masters at having fun.

Then, all of sudden we get older, wiser, smarter. As adults we become less spontaneous. We plan everything. We plan work time and play time. We even plan when to make a plan. We then look at children having an exciting, spontaneous, fun time; we sigh and say, "Oh, to be young again."

Sara was a busy mom and a community volunteer. In addition to keeping up with her family responsibilities, she volunteered at a shelter for abused women one morning a week. Sara was on several community boards, she belonged to two book clubs, and she took a class at the community college. She was one busy lady!

Sara hired us because she was very stressed and no longer having fun. We asked her to think of a time when she really enjoyed each day. As our coaching progressed, Sara considered eliminating those activities that were no longer bringing her joy. She chose to discontinue one of her book clubs and went off one community board. These two actions alone freed up her time to have more fun with her current activities.

So, are you having fun yet? As you think and plan, are you focusing on what's fun? If your answer is no, you are missing a great opportunity.

Make a commitment not to outlive your childhood. Start your fun game each morning. Each challenge will become an opportunity for more fun. You will have endless energy day in and day out. You won't get bored. You will be motivated to get up and go for it. You will probably earn more than you ever dreamed possible. Most important of all, you will be happy and you will radiate your positive feelings to everyone around you.

"I wake up laughing every day. I get a kick out of life."
—Bruce Willis

"People rarely succeed unless they have fun in what they are doing."
—Dale Carnegie

Research has shown that employees having fun are more productive. Finding the fun in everything tends to help lower blood pressure. Families having fun together seem to stay together. The list goes on and on. Take a quick look at yourself.

Describe the fun things about your job.

_____
_____
_____
_____
_____
_____

Describe the fun things about your family.

_____
_____
_____
_____
_____

Describe the fun things you do just for the fun of it.

_____
_____
_____
_____
_____

Do you want to attract more fun into your life? Look for the possibilities for fun in each moment. Guess what? The possibilities are everywhere.

Secret Number Sixteen

Expect Good Luck

Discover that

The BETTER It Gets!

The BETTER It Gets!

The BETTER It Gets!

Since you attract what you think about, where will you focus?

Jackie Gleason described life like this: *"How Sweeeet It Is!"*

Make This Your Lucky Day

Remember that day when everything was perfect? You had positive momentum. Everything you touched turned into something good. If you were a golfer, on that day you were the master of your sport. Your shots were long and accurate. Your putts were right on the money. If you were a salesperson, everyone said yes. As a CEO, your company was profitable in all areas. As a manager, your people were motivated and productive. As a parent, your family was in complete harmony. How well you remember that totally lucky day. On that day, your life was truly a celebration.

Now think about the other kind of day. You know what that was like. Nothing seemed to go quite right. The harder you tried, the worse it got. On that day, even your favorite chocolate didn't taste so good.

What can you now do to have more of those lucky days? You can create your own luck and here's how to do it. According to psychologist Richard Wiseman, these four principles can create good fortune in your life and your career.

1. **Maximize Chance Opportunities.** Lucky people are skilled at creating, noticing, and acting upon chance opportunities.

2. **Listen to Your Lucky Hunches.** Lucky people make effective decisions by listening to their intuition and gut feelings.

3. **Expect Good Fortune.** Lucky people are certain that the future will be bright. Over time that expectation becomes a self-fulfilling prophesy.

4. **Turn Bad Luck into Good.** Lucky people imagine how things could have been worse. They don't dwell on their ill fortune. They take control of the situation.

Start now to develop the mindset of a very lucky person. Begin by taking inventory of how lucky you are right now.

Think about the people in your life that you love and who love you.
Lucky you!
Think about all the parts of your body that are working well.
Lucky you!
Think about the opportunities you have in your career.
Lucky you!
Add to your list every day.

Oops, life throws you a curve and you strike out. Now what? You've heard the saying, "If life gives you lemons, make lemonade." That's the mindset of a very lucky person. As you continue to think about how lucky you are, even in very small ways, you will begin to realize that the possibilities for luck abound everywhere. You will begin to be more aware as you ask yourself, "How can I make lemonade out of this situation?" Keep looking for good luck and you will move from where you are to where you want to be.

This is a good time to put yourself on the Good Luck Fast Track. Appreciate what you have now and expect it to get better. You can become a "GOOD LUCK" magnet. Of course, that means, The Better It Gets! The Better It Gets! The Better It Gets!

"May your pockets be heavy and your heart be light. May good luck pursue you each morning and night."—Irish Blessing

How good can your life really be? Using your wildest imagination, write a description of how good you want your life to be.

_____

_____

_____

_____

_____

_____

_____

_____

Lucky You!

Secret Number Seventeen

The Power of Slowing Down

"Slow down and enjoy life. It's not only the scenery you miss by going too fast; you also miss the sense of where you are going and why."—Eddie Cantor

"There is more to life than increasing its speed."—Mahatma Gandhi

"Rest is not idleness, and to lie sometimes on the grass under trees on a summer's day, listening to the murmur of the water, or watching the clouds float across the sky, is by no means a waste of time."—J. Lubbock

"It's not how fast you go; it's being there."
—Richard Bach

The Power of Slowing Down

It seems that time goes by faster than ever before. We live in a speed worshipping society. We can send an e-mail anywhere in an instant. We look for faster ways to do everything. A survey taken in New York City showed these kinds of results to the question: "Where are you going in such a hurry?" The typical answers were, "I'm going to lunch." "I'm taking a relaxing walk; no place special." Many of us are in a hurry and don't even know it.

Remember the movie, *Groundhog Day?* Every day was the same old hectic thing. Rachel, a client of ours, hired us as her coach for that very reason. Her story was typical of many. She awoke at 5:30 every morning and got ready for work. She prepared breakfast for the family and got the kids to school on time. At 8 AM she's in the office and on the phone with clients. Rachel perfected her multitasking and does many things very quickly. By 5 PM, she's back in traffic and home for the evening activities. At 5:30 the next morning, here she goes again.

Rachel felt she was on a speedy treadmill going nowhere. Of course, there are times when speed and immediate action are essential. However, slowing down, seeing the big picture, and enjoying the trip are vital.

Rachel began to change her daily routine and became more productive. She found little slivers of time to relax. She found that often less is more. She became in charge of her schedule instead of being a victim of her routine.

Chasing goals often gets us worked up to the point that we are more passionate about the future than we are about the present. Hit the pause button on your mental computer. Choose to cross a few things off your to-do list that you really don't have to do. It's like magic. You just moved closer to your goal without any effort. To slow down, learn the lost art of strolling. Wander with no particular place to go. Take a deep breath and see the wonder of where you are now.

*"Slow down and everything you are chasing
will come around and catch you."*—John DePaola

Slooooow Down

Be present in this moment. Slow down. Really slow down. Look around the room and search for things you have never really focused on before. "That's a very interesting picture." "There's a book I love; I should read it again." "This is a great wood floor."

Take inventory of all the stuff you feel you must get done. Ask yourself, "What's the worst thing that could happen if I just put it off for a few hours or even a day?" When you choose to have "Slow Down Time" in your life, you will:

Feel renewed. See what's really important. Have less stress. Know yourself better.

Take five minutes right now to focus on this moment.

What do you see? _____

What do you hear? _____

What do you feel? _____

What do you like about your new awareness?

_____

_____

_____

_____

_____

Secret Number Eighteen

Procrastination is the Silent Killer

Ask yourself:

"What is the worst thing that could happen to me if I did what I'm putting off?" The answer is usually so insignificant that it could jar you into action.

Think about this:

Now is the only time you ever have.
Delaying anything makes no sense.

"Nothing is so fatiguing as the eternal hanging on of an uncompleted task."
—William James

Procrastination is the Silent Killer

These thoughts will kill the most powerful ideas: *I'll do it later. I'll do it tomorrow. I'll do it when I feel better. I'll do it when the time is right. When I make my New Year's resolutions, then I'll get into action.* Procrastination is considered the art of keeping up with yesterday.

The habit of procrastination is the one habit—more than any other—that puts the brakes on achievement. Psychologists, business and sales trainers, coaches, and educators have examined it and have created hundreds of solutions. Most of these solutions do not work because people procrastinate putting them into action.

Procrastinators put off doing what they feel they should be doing because they anticipate a negative result. They imagine what others will think of them. They get that feeling that says, "Not now, later." You know when later comes. Never! So is there hope? Of course.

Here are some strategies that have worked well for many of our clients:

A. Know what you want and why you want it. If you want more money, ask yourself why that is important. What will you do with it? How will it make you feel? Reminding yourself of these answers will make taking action easy.

B. Clear the clutter. Clutter will create the illusion that you are overworked. When you clear the clutter, your mind is free to take on important actions.

C. Don't beat yourself up when you procrastinate. It's okay not to do something. That in itself is a choice. Next, you can choose something else. Remember, you are in charge.

D. Keep it simple. Time management consultant, Alan Lakein, recommends the Swiss Cheese Method. He suggests making holes in that big job with little instant tasks that take ten minutes or less. You can do anything for just ten minutes. By taking bite size pieces, the job will be completed.

E. Take care of your health. When you are really ill or exhausted, don't expect to be a peak performer. Even small tasks will seem insurmountable. Remember the basics: Eat well, exercise daily, and get enough sleep. When you take care of your health, you will maintain the energy needed to "Do It Now" when the procrastination feeling creeps in.

"Waiting is a trap. There will always be reasons to wait. The truth is, there are only two things in life, reasons and results, and reasons simply don't count."
—Dr. Robert Anthony

"I looked and looked and could not find the secret to success. So I went on without it and found it."—Jonathan Winters

So What Actions Are You Going To Take?

Take a moment now and list five actions that you have been putting off. Then list the benefits you will receive by taking action now.

1. _____

   _____

2. _____

   _____

3. _____

   _____

4. _____

   _____

5. _____

   _____

"Success is simple: Do what's right, the right way, at the right time."
—Arnold H. Glasgow

Secret Number Nineteen

Raise Your E.Q.
Your Enthusiasm Quotient

Is it Low? Medium? High? Unstoppable?

Ralph Waldo Emerson tells us:
"Nothing great was ever achieved without enthusiasm."

Be Bold! Speak Up! Stand Tall!
Move Quickly! Smile Often!

"Think big. Settle for more."—Joseph Campbell

Fire Up Your Life with Enthusiasm

Imagine this: It is next month already. The previous month has zipped by with lightning speed. The month was filled with success after success. New ideas came to you daily. New people became interested in your plans. Your challenges seemed to melt away. You had one happy surprise after another. You felt physically strong and mentally sharp. You were unstoppable.

How can you make this happen for you consistently? There is only one thing blocking this outcome. It's something we all have total control over every moment of our lives. It's our EQ, our Enthusiasm Quotient. What is your quotient? On a scale from one to ten, how enthusiastic are you about your career, your family, your future, yourself?

Susan felt bogged down, tired, and overwhelmed. She felt she needed rest and took the day off work to sleep. When she awoke, she felt great until she thought about the challenge facing her. What happened? She went right back to feeling bogged down, tired, and overwhelmed. Seemed like a no-win situation, right? We asked Susan what specifically was making her feel that way. She replied, "This week I have to handle a complaint from one of our best clients. I really don't want to talk with this person because I'm not certain I will be able to resolve the problem."

As we coached Susan, she began to see that what was making her feel bogged down and tired was resistance. She then realized she had another choice. As soon as Susan began to focus on the benefits of taking action instead of the possibllity of failure, her enthusiasm began to rise. She began to feel better about herself and her career. Enthusiastic action replaced resistance.

How about the challenges in your life? Do you put on your enthusiasm hat and plunge right in, or do you test the water a hundred ways first? Do you say, "I wonder what exciting possibilities I'll find in this situation? Or do you say, "Oh no, do I really have to do this?"

When you have enthusiasm, wonderful possibilities appear. In the words of Johann Wolfgang von Goethe, "*All sorts of things occur to help one that would never otherwise have occurred. A whole stream of events issue from the decision, raising in one's favor all manner of unforeseen incidents, meetings, and material assistance which no man could have dreamed would have come his way.*"

"The minute you begin to do what you want to do, it's a different kind of life."—Buckminster Fuller

MAKE TODAY YOUR DAY!

There is plenty to be excited about in our world today. Think about this:

TODAY … there are more opportunities than ever before!

TODAY … millions of people are getting new jobs!

TODAY … millions of people are being promoted!

TODAY … millions of people are acquiring huge amounts of money!

TODAY … millions of people are getting married!

TODAY … millions of healthy babies are being born!

TODAY … millions of people are attaining their ideal weight!

TODAY … millions of people are living their dream lives!

What am I going to be enthusiastic about today?

_____

_____

_____

_____

_____

_____

_____

_____

_____

_____

Secret Number Twenty

Clear the Clutter

Do you have a lot of clutter in your life?
Would you like to clear it away?
What benefit would you gain?

You will think more clearly.
You will have more energy.
You will worry less.
You will feel free.

"When what you want is clear, the how will appear."
—Author Unknown

Clear the Clutter for Clarity

It's a time for renewal, which means clearing away the clutter. Take a look around. Where did all of this stuff come from? It's time to clear the clutter from your mental and physical world.

Mark, our coaching client, had wonderful goals that he had committed to in January, but because he was confronted with so much clutter, he was unable to stay on track. Papers began to pile up everywhere. His organized filing system was no more. His closets were filled with clothes he hadn't worn in years.

Mark became immobilized, unable to make a decision. Should he join a health club in order to lose those ten pounds? Should he keep the new TV that was too expensive? Should he expand his business? What to do?

We suggested to Mark that he stop all activity and reconnect with his goals. We also suggested he eliminate everything that did not move him closer to his goals, one item at a time. He discarded hundreds of papers and old files. He donated clothing he no longer needed. He returned the expensive TV. He joined the health club. He began to relax. He was back on track with his decision-making.

Clearing clutter can transform your life by releasing negative emotions and generating energy. This allows you to create space in your life for the things you really want.

What is clutter anyway?

Clutter is stuff in your home or life that no longer brings any benefit.

Clutter is whatever requires more of your time than it is worth.

Clutter is that which you don't need or use.

Clutter is what you keep because of some obligation, rather than because you want it.

Clutter is anything you own that does not improve the quality of your life.

Clutter is the fruit of your procrastination.

Does your home or office environment bring you feelings of peace or feelings of stress?

All of a sudden there it is. So much stuff to look through. So much to do. How do I wade through all of this? One word describes how clutter is created, and that word is **indecision.**

"Clutter drains your energy, and you don't realize it till it's gone. Every item in your home or office has an energy to it. When items go a long time unused, unloved, and uncared for, they become stuck, stagnant energy that actually physically drains you of your energy."—Ariane Benefit

Three Rules of Life by Albert Einstein
1. Out of clutter find simplicity
2. From discord find harmony
3. In the middle of difficulty lies opportunity

Think simplify, simplify, simplify! List the things you can give away, discard, or organize, and write down when you are going to do it.

_____

_____

_____

_____

_____

_____

_____

_____

_____

_____

Secret Number Twenty-One

Shelve Those Worries

Worrying is using your imagination to create
something you do not want.

Set aside a time slot exclusively for worry. How about 7:00 to
7:15 every evening?

When a worry thought arises, tell yourself, "Now is not the
time." You may actually forget to worry at all.

"Worry never robs tomorrow of its sorrow, it only saps today of its joy."
—Leo Buscaglia

The Worry of Living in a Chaotic World

Every day people are telling us to have a good day. Have you ever had thoughts like these: "Don't tell me to have a good day. You've got to be kidding! Have you checked the news lately? More Americans killed in Iraq. Threat of global warming increases. More droughts in the Midwest. Planned airline bombings discovered in London. The West Nile Virus is coming our way. The deadly bird flu is a possibility."

Some of our coaching clients ask us, "How can I feel free to enjoy my life and pursue my dreams when so many people in the world are experiencing violence and death?"

Hold on. Take a deep breath. What if you had not heard or read about these topics? Would the possibility of having a good day improve? So it's not the event that makes you feel bad; it's what you do with the image in your mind.

Ask yourself this question: "Would I rather be free, or would I rather be stuck, thinking about all the pain and uncertainly in the world?" Many of our clients discover that they can let go of the feelings that are not serving them and still be able to make the world a better place. They do this by making their own lives better first. Here's the key: Focus on thoughts that make you feel good. Make a list and check it often.

The benefits of really feeling good:
When you are Really Feeling Good, your worries disappear.
When you are Really Feeling Good, you have more energy.
When you are Really Feeling Good, people are attracted to you.
When you are Really Feeling Good, you actually look better.
When you are Really Feeling Good, your problems are easily solved.
When you are Really Feeling Good, you get things done more quickly.
When you are Really Feeling Good, you will be more naturally relaxed.
When you are Really Feeling Good, you attract your goals and dreams.

What's the best time to feel good and be happy? In the words of Deepak Chopra, *"Keep your attention on this moment. This moment is the only moment you have the power to act. You can not take action in the past or future, so if you dwell in the past or the future, you feel powerless. Life/happiness is in this moment. When the future happens, it happens now. The present is the only moment that never ends."*

This moment is your life. What are you going to do in it? When someone says to you, "Have a good day," how will you respond? How about this: "Of course, I already am! Thank you!"

"Don't Worry, Be Happy."
—Bobby McFerrin

Did you know that it is impossible to worry and to feel good at the same time? When you allow yourself to worry, you attract more of it into your life. The other people around you then do the same thing. Let's focus now on what makes you feel great.

When I think THIS I feel great:

_____

_____

_____

Go ahead and brainstorm more feel-good thoughts that you can focus on whenever worry creeps in. Write those thoughts here.

_____

_____

_____

_____

_____

_____

_____

_____

_____

_____

Secret Number Twenty-Two

Get Off Your Buts

Yes, I want to live my dreams, BUT ...
Yes, I want to reduce the clutter in my life, BUT ...
Yes, I must take steps to improve my relationships, BUT ...
Yes, I need to lose twenty pounds and I want to start now, BUT ...

Remember the truth about yourself:
You are capable and competent. You have within you everything you
will ever need to make your life exactly the way you want it to be.

When a "Yes, But" thought appears,
hit your mental "delete button" and move on.

"Everything you want is out there waiting for you. Everything you want also wants you. But you have to take action to get it."—Jack Canfield

Yes, It's Time to Get Off Your Buts!

You have a clear idea of what you really want. As you move toward it, do you sometimes fail to take action because your life is full of thoughts like, "I should do it, but." "It's a good idea, but."

We all have limiting beliefs that stop us from doing what we want to do. Here are some examples: "I can't sing; I think I'm tone deaf." "I can't dance; I have no coordination." "Golf is not for me; I could never hit that ball." "Go back to school? No way, I was never that great a student." "Run for office? I don't have what it takes." "Lose forty pounds? I've lost and gained hundreds over the years." "Run a marathon? In the shape I'm in, forget it." "Find a life partner? I can't; must be something wrong with me."

These kinds of thoughts and feelings silently prevent us from living our life on our terms. Many of us decide to settle for less because that's the way life is. Or is it? Is your belief empowering or limiting? If it is limiting, change that belief and your "Yes, Buts" will be just YES.

Do this:
1. Choose to believe that what you want is possible.
2. Think about how you will feel when what you want is yours.
3. Take one baby step toward your goal and act as if it is already yours.

Ralph Waldo Emerson said, *"Belief follows action, not the other way around."*

Sam Walton, with very little retail experience, purchased a failed Ben Franklin store. He didn't say, "I'd like to succeed, but I have no experience." He started taking steps toward his dream. The result: Wal-Mart.

Rose Blumkin, a penniless immigrant, had plenty of reasons to use the "Yes, But" excuse. Instead she moved with total belief as she created America's largest and most profitable family-owned furniture store, the Nebraska Furniture Mart in Omaha, Nebraska.

Fred Astaire was told by Warner Brothers that he couldn't act, was too skinny, and could dance a little. No "Yes, But" for him.

Walt Disney was fired from the *Los Angeles Times* for having too little imagination. He kept on keeping on. If he would have said, "Yes, But," we would all have been denied Disney World.

Some of our clients brought their "Yes, Buts" to our coaching sessions. They have then gone on to become highly successful in their personal and professional lives. You can do the same. No more "Yes, Buts." Just say YES to life.

"You can have anything you want if you will give up the belief that you can't have it."—Dr. Robert Anthony

Nothing Happens Until We Get Off Our Buts

Think of one idea you said yes to and imagined the many benefits the idea could produce. Then you thought, *"I really want to do this ...*

***BUT** I'm a little short on cash.*
***BUT** I'm just too tired.*
***BUT** I'm just not sure I have the ability.*

As you know, BUT is simply an excuse for not taking action.

What one action step can you take this week that will move you closer to your goal? Choose an action that takes you out of your comfort zone.

_____
_____
_____
_____
_____

What is the benefit to you when you move past the YES, BUT and get into action?

_____
_____
_____
_____
_____

Secret Number Twenty-Three

The Magic of Letting Go

Letting Go of the Feeling of Fear will leave you with courage.
Letting Go of the Feeling of Doubt will leave you with confidence.
Letting Go of the Feeling of Stress will leave you with peace.
Letting Go of the Feeling of Sadness will leave you with happiness.

Instead of trying to resist your negative feelings, simply welcome them and then let them go. When you resist them, you reinforce what you do not want.

"We must be willing to let go, so as to accept the life that is waiting for us."—Joseph Campbell

The Magic of Letting Go

It's Monday morning. You awaken, look at the clock, and realize that you have overslept. Unless you hurry, you will be late for an important appointment. You feel the stress coming on. You hurry to your car. You start driving and ask yourself questions like: "What's wrong with me, anyway?" "How could I allow myself to oversleep?" A hurried feeling comes over you, but very soon a change occurs. You begin to feel yourself relaxing as you go through one green light after another. What a relief; all green lights, no road construction, and most of all, no stress.

What if you could create a green light path to your goals every day? Where are these goals and dreams that you feel will make your life complete? Of course, they are in your mind, in your thinking process. What if it were possible to let go of the feelings holding you back?

Our client Andrew said, "I have to lose weight. I look in the mirror and see an unhealthy person that I do not like." He went on to say, "I want to get my finances in order. I make a great income and I'm still overextended. I get completely stressed out when I can't pay all my bills, and I can never save anything." We said, "Andrew, listen to the words you are using."

His words were creating red lights on the path to his goals. He was telling himself that he was a person with lack and frustration. When we focus on those thoughts, we get more of what we don't want.

We asked Andrew to think about how he could change those red lights to green lights. After a few coaching sessions, he said, "I may be my own worst enemy." Together we brainstormed a strategy to let go of what was not working for him.

Andrew soon got excited and motivated. He started thinking about what was necessary for him to reach his ideal weight. Instead of complaining, he began thinking about solutions. It was the same with his finances. He began taking actions that produced the results he wanted. There was no more "poor me" talk. Whenever he faced a problem, he put himself on a mental green light path.

Simply let go of the feelings of fear, doubt, stress, frustration, and sadness. You will be left with courage, confidence, peace, calm, and happiness. These thoughts will give you a feeling of well being. Other people will notice and will draw themselves to you.

"When you simply let go of your imaginary restraints,
you will no longer resist moving freely to your dream."
—Author Unknown

The Magic of Letting Go

Move from Red Light Thinking to Green Light Thinking. You will be on a clear path to what you really want. Select an area of your life that you want to improve. Under the Red Light Thinking column list what you don't like about your life; under the Green Light Thinking column write the way you want your life to be. You will begin to attract whichever you focus on with feeling.

RED LIGHT THINKING	**GREEN LIGHT THINKING**
Example: I don't like the way my boss speaks to me.	Example: I choose to have a good relationship with my boss.

1.

2.

3.

4.

To release those red light feelings and thoughts:
Locate in your body the feeling that you want to release. Often it is felt in the abdomen. Focus on the feeling and welcome it. As soon as you welcome the feeling, there is no more resistance and you are in control. Now take five deep breaths, and with each exhale, visualize the feeling leaving your body and mind. You will soon feel free to live your life with productive Green Light Thinking.

Secret Number Twenty-Four

Take Time to Do Nothing

Did you ever see a dog chase his tail? No matter how fast he goes, his tail always eludes him. He finally relaxes, lies down, and there it is. His tail is right there before him.

Five Minutes Can Make a Huge Difference.

For five minutes, relax under an oak tree and listen to the birds.
For five minutes, sit in a chair and breathe slow and easy.
For five minutes, look at your favorite photo album.

"No matter how much pressure you feel, if you could find ways to relax for at least five minutes every hour, you'd be more productive and happier."
—Dr. Joyce Brothers

Doing Nothing is Not a Waste of Time

It's time to take a breath. Stop all activity, clear your mind, and get into the moment. Regardless of the month you are reading this, ask yourself this question: In the last twelve months did I focus on my goals until they were completed? This question could be embarrassing. Many of us did not even come close to our intentions and we sacrificed today's happiness by feeling guilty about it. Don't feel bad if this applies to you. Most New Year's resolutions are never acted upon.

Why does this happen to most of us in some degree? Many times the goals we choose are not our own. Some of us live our lives to satisfy other people more than ourselves. Perhaps the goals we choose have lost luster. The excitement is gone. Yet, we keep on moving toward something we no longer really want. We actually set ourselves up for failure. It's difficult to keep striving for something for which you no longer have positive feelings.

The next twelve months can be refreshing and magical for you. It can be a time of adventure, a time when everything comes together and your life takes on new meaning, excitement, and passion. So, let go of the stuff that has not worked and take time to simply do nothing.

Now with your relaxed mindset, you begin to realize that life is continuing without your hurried actions. Reflect on these four points before you resume reaching for your dreams.

1. Be easy on yourself. Make a commitment to enjoy each step, successful or not. Move with passion in the direction of your goal, one day at a time.

2. Realize that you are never lost, even if you feel off track. Every wrong move is an opportunity to experience new things and new possibilities to make your goal even more desirable.

3. Stay in the present moment. Every morning take time to write down what you appreciate in your life right now. Remind yourself that where you are is where you need to be.

4. Seek out a new adventure often. It will keep you feeling alive.

"Relaxation means releasing all concern and tension and letting the natural order of life flow through one's being."—Donald Curtis

Take Five Now!

Take this moment to free your mind. Take three deep breaths. Inhale and exhale slowly. Now take three more. Close your eyes and imagine a peaceful place. Let all the have to's, shoulds, gotta do it nows, go. Just let it go. This is your place. No one else is admitted. Visualize a sandy beach with a gentle breeze. Listen to the seagulls overhead. Smell the fresh air. Relax into this vision and ignore the thoughts that cause you to hurry. Sit quietly and let your muscles relax, one at a time. Are you letting go? Let go a little more. Now just a little more.

Allow yourself to focus on your dream. Bring it into your awareness without any thought of taking action. You feel good in your special place. Whatever you want is yours. See it. Hear the sounds that surround it. Sense the feeling of knowing it's yours. Remain in relaxed silence for a few moments, alone with your dream. Gently say to yourself, "This is mine" as you let go … let go … let go … let go. Just breathe slowly for a few minutes. Excellent. Now take a deep breath and close your imaginary door to your private place. Allow yourself to begin your activities. You can return at any time.

Secret Number Twenty-Five

Your Attitude is Everything

What is your attitude as you approach this day?

"There is little difference in people, but that little difference makes a big difference. The little difference is attitude. The big difference is whether it is positive or negative."—W. Clement Stone

"Attitude is a little thing that makes a big difference."
—Winston Churchill

Your Attitude Paves Your Way to Success

We have been told that attitude is everything. Is it really? Is everything we do successfully or unsuccessfully based on our attitude? The famous psychologist William James said, *"The greatest discovery of my generation is that human beings can alter their lives by altering their attitudes of mind."*

That's great advice. But, how do we know if we need a change in attitude? If you are not living the kind of life that brings you satisfaction, joy, and abundance, jump on the "Attitude Change Band Wagon" now.

Ponder this: When we change how we think about something, the thing we are thinking about changes. (Please read this sentence again.)

It's easy to say, "Change your attitude and change your life," but how do we do that and how easy is it? The good news is that it does not have to be difficult if you use a few proven strategies. If you desire to be happier, have more abundance, and less stress, why not try these simple techniques?

Think of people you know who have a great attitude. They are probably upbeat, they think in terms of possibilities, they are non-critical, they laugh often, and they are great to be around. You now have role models.

Check your attitude with the "mirror technique." Observe the attitudes of the people around you. If they are less than open, a little down, or grumpy, that could be a reflection of your attitude. Attitudes are contagious.

Think with the end in mind. See yourself as that joyful, upbeat, successful person you are on your way to becoming. Understand that whatever you need to live your dreams is already here.

Stop taking yourself so seriously. Look for the humor in all situations.

Remember that things take time. In many cases you will get immediate results, but if you don't, DO NOT GIVE UP. It will come.

If you are not getting the results you want in any area of your life, do an attitude check on yourself. Even better, have a friend give you some feedback on how you come across to others. This kind of knowledge is power. You can now flip the attitude switch to ON and change how you look at things so the things that you look at will change. You will then have an endless supply of green lights before you.

"I take nothing for granted. I now have only good days or great days."
—Lance Armstrong

What you are thinking in this moment creates what you are feeling. What you are feeling is your current attitude. It's the spirit in which you do things.

Try this experiment:

If you want to attract negative, undesirable things into your life, think about something that makes you sad. Go into a droop mode and put a sad expression on your face. How do you feel? It's easy to go into a negative place, isn't it?

Yes! You can choose your attitude in any given moment. Describe one positive change you will make in your attitude today.

_____

_____

_____

_____

_____

_____

_____

**Your positive attitude is the engine that will take you
where you want to go.**

"Everything happens in a moment. Make this moment yours!"—Wayne Dyer

Why Not Go Ahead Now?

Why Not—Go Ahead and Dream Big?
"If you dream it you can do it."—Walt Disney

Why Not—Go Ahead and Believe You Can?
"Whether you think you can or think you can't—you are right."—Henry Ford

Why Not—Go Ahead and Try?
"You miss 100 percent of the shots you don't take."—Wayne Gretzky

Why Not—Go Ahead and Refuse to Give Up?
"The most important things in the world have been accomplished by people who have kept on trying when there seemed to be no hope at all."—Dale Carnegie

Why Not—Go Ahead and Lighten Up?
"You grow up the day you have the first real laugh ... at yourself."
—Ethel Barrymore

Pulling It All Together

My Script for Living My Dreams

My Name_____

I am capable of living my life on my terms. I have many positive qualities
that include_____
_____
_____
_____

I have thought long and hard about what I really, really, really want for
myself. When I visualize my goal,

I see_____
_____

I hear_____
_____

I taste_____
_____

I feel_____
_____

Whenever I get off track and my thoughts and actions stop bringing me what I want, I immediately refocus on what I am grateful for in my present moments. I deeply appreciate:

_____

_____

_____

_____

_____

_____

When I focus with feeling on what I appreciate, I begin to attract more of the same. I'm developing the habit of saying:

YES, to life.
YES, to abundance.
YES, to vibrant good health.
YES, to harmonious relationships.
YES, to my ability to live my dream life.

I know that ultimately I will have _____

_____

I have decided to _____

I love the idea of _____

I'm excited at the thought of _____

I can't wait until I _____

We Totally Believe In You!

Live Your Dream Now!

We want you to live your dream life now, and we would be honored to be a part of your progress. One way to stay motivated is to visit our Web site at **www.KenyonCoaching.com** and sign up for Fire Up Your Week. You will then receive our FREE 30-second infusion of positive energy in your e-mail every Monday morning. Your Monday mornings will be better than ever!

A surprising thing happens when you work with a coach.
You have someone totally committed to your success and well-being.
You have someone who wants for you what you want for yourself.
You have someone to be a sounding board for you.
You have someone to encourage you when you need a boost.
You have someone who holds your vision if you temporarily lose it.
You have someone who is eager to celebrate your success with you.

Who hires a coach?
Just as serious athletes hire coaches, so do motivated people in other walks of life. Entrepreneurs, business leaders, professionals, salespeople, college students, retirees, and people in transition typically work with a coach. Regardless of their place in life, our clients have one thing in common: They are all success-minded, resourceful, and intelligent individuals who are ready to go for the things they really want in their lives.

Why does coaching work?

When you and your coach work as a team committed to your goals, a positive energy is created and results come quickly. Coaching works because you are now performing actions that get desired results. All coaching is completely confidential.

Tiger Woods is one of the best golfers and yet he understands the value that comes from having a coach. His coach points out things Tiger can't see, and keeps encouraging and challenging him. When you have Kenyon Coaching on your team, it's like having a personal trainer for your life!

"If you always do what you've always done, you'll always get what you've always got."—Anonymous

---

Fire Up Your Life Now!
Workshop

Kenyon Coaching presents a powerful interactive workshop designed to motivate people into action by applying the twenty-five secrets in this book. Please contact Kenyon Coaching today for information on how your organization can benefit from this workshop and schedule it for your next conference or retreat. Desired results are only one phone call away.

Complimentary 30-Minute
Telephone Coaching Consultation

Kenyon Coaching offers Personal and Business Coaching for individuals who feel stuck and want to jump-start their life. Our coaching is done by telephone and is totally confidential. If you want to move more quickly to your goals, please take advantage of our complimentary consultation. It's a great way to experience the benefit of having a life coach and there is absolutely no obligation.

Kenyon Coaching
(402) 423-6777
www.KenyonCoaching.com

"We coach our clients to develop
a passionate sense of what's possible."

About Allan and Barbara Kenyon

Allan and Barbara Kenyon are personal and business coaches dedicated to helping individuals and businesses reach their goals through Attraction Based Coaching.

Allan was a certified instructor/coach with Dale Carnegie Training for twenty years, and owner/trainer for Seminar Training Systems. He has been trained in neuro-linguistic programming by NLP Comprehensive, and he received coach training with Coach Training Institute. Allan is passionate about helping his clients move quickly to the life they envision for themselves.

Barbara, a graduate of Coach U, the leading global provider of coach training programs, is a certified coach with the International Coach Federation. She holds a master's degree in counseling. Barbara is a natural coach who has a gift for getting in tune with her clients. Nothing gives her greater joy than to see her clients reach their goals and their dreams.

Kenyon Coaching is a member of the International Coach Federation

Before We Say Good-bye

We thank you so much for reading *Fire Up Your Life Now!* You have experienced the *Secrets* that can help you move swiftly to the life you really want. Promise yourself to review the Secrets that resonate with you. The more you act on them, the happier and more productive your life can become.

We genuinely care about your success. Please e-mail us at the address below and let us know how your life has become more fired up since reading our book. We would love to hear from you!

Here's to your living a Fired Up Life!

Allan and Barbara Kenyon
AttractSuccess@KenyonCoaching.com

Recommended Reading

Ask and It Is Given, by Jerry and Esther Hicks

Age of Speed, by Vince Poscente

The Aladdin Factor, by Jack Canfield and Mark Victor Hansen

The Attractor Factor, by Joe Vitale

The Art of Possibility, by Benjamin Zander

The Greatest Salesman in the World, by Og Mandino

How to Win Friends and Influence People, by Dale Carnegie

How Full is Your Bucket? by Donald Clifton and Tom Rath

Inspiration, by Dr. Wayne Dyer

Law of Attraction, by Michael Losier

The Luck Factor, by Dr. Richard Wiseman

The Magic of Thinking Big, by Dr. David Schwartz

Notes from the Universe, by Mike Dooley

The Pleasure Prescription, by Paul Pearsall

The Power of Intention, by Dr. Wayne Dyer

The Power of the Subconscious Mind, by Dr. Joseph Murphy

The Power of Now, by Eckhart Tolle

Power vs. Force, by David Hawkins

The Secret, by Rhonda Byrne

The Sedona Method, by Hale Dwoskin

Success—The Original Hand Book, by Joey Reiman

Think and Grow Rich, by Napoleon Hill

The Unmistakable Touch of Grace, by Cheryl Richardson

Zero Limits, by Joe Vitale and Ihaleakala Hew Len, PhD

978-0-595-43514-2
0-595-43514-9

Printed in the United States
110183LV00002B/1-165/P